Blessed Are the Refugees

# Blessed Are the Refugees

## *Beatitudes of Immigrant Children*

*Stories by Staff and Volunteers of
Catholic Charities' Esperanza Center*

Scott Rose
Mikhael H. Borgonos
Andrea Naft
Cary Plamondon
Val Twanmoh

With a Foreword by Joe Biden
Preface and Prayers by Leo J. O'Donovan, S.J.
Illustrations by Ana Silvia Herrera Delgado and
Jose Enrique Portillo Delgado

ORBIS BOOKS
**Maryknoll, New York 10545**

Founded in 1970, Orbis Books endeavors to publish works that enlighten the mind, nourish the spirit, and challenge the conscience. The publishing arm of the Maryknoll Fathers and Brothers, Orbis seeks to explore the global dimensions of the Christian faith and mission, to invite dialogue with diverse cultures and religious traditions, and to serve the cause of reconciliation and peace. The books published reflect the views of their authors and do not represent the official position of the Maryknoll Society. To learn more about Maryknoll and Orbis Books, please visit our website at www.maryknollsociety.org.

Throughout this book, all references to Esperaanza or the Esperanza Center refer to Catholic Charities of Baltimore's Esperanza Center, located in Fells Point, Baltimore, Maryland. To the best of the authors' ability, they have re-created events, locales, people, and organizations from their memories of them. In order to maintain the anonymity of others, in most instances, the authors have changed the names of individuals and places, and the details of events.

Manufactured in the United States of America.

Library of Congress Cataloging-in-Publication Data
Names: Rose, Scott (CEO), author.
Title: Blessed are the refugees : beatitudes of immigrant children / Scott
    Rose, Mikhael H. Borgonos, Andrea Naft, Cary Plamondon, Val Twanmoh.
Description: Maryknoll : Orbis Books, 2018.
Identifiers: LCCN 2018008299 (print) | ISBN 9781626982888 )pbk.)
Subjects: LCSH: Church work with regfugees. | Church work with children |
    Catholic Church—Charities | Refugee children—Central America—
    Biography. | Refugee children—Prayers and devotions
Classification: LCC BX2347.8.R44 B54 2018 (print)
    | DDC 261.5/328083—dc23
LC record anailable at https://lccn.loc.gov/2018008299

*In Memory of*

*Rev. Pedro Arrupe, S.J.,*
*founder of Jesuit Refugee Service*

*Sr. Mary Neil Corcoran, R.S.M.,*
*director of Esperanza Center for over twenty years*

*Adan Guevara Martinez,*
*who worked in the shadows to give light to others*

## The Beatitudes

*Blessed Are the Poor in Spirit*
*for Theirs Is the Kingdom of Heaven*

*Blessed Are They Who Mourn*
*for They Shall Be Comforted*

*Blessed Are the Meek*
*for They Shall Inherit the Earth*

*Blessed Are They Who Hunger and Thirst for Righteousness*
*for They Shall Be Satisfied*

*Blessed Are the Merciful*
*for They Shall Receive Mercy*

*Blessed Are the Pure of Heart*
*for They Shall See God*

*Blessed Are the Peacemakers*
*for They Shall Be Called Children of God*

*Blessed Are They Who Are Persecuted*
*for the Sake of Righteousness*
*for Theirs Is the Kingdom of Heaven*

# Contents

Foreword / Joe Biden
**xi**

Preface / Is God Watching?
Leo J. O'Donovan, S.J.
**xiii**

Introduction / Scott Rose
*Prayer: "Where True Happiness Can Be Found"*
**xx**

Blessed Are the Poor in Spirit for Theirs Is the Kingdom
of Heaven / Scott Rose
Artwork / Jose Enrique Portillo Delgado
*Prayer: "Simple Trust in God"*
**1**

Blessed Are They Who Mourn for They Shall Be
Comforted / Andrea Naft
Artwork / Ana Silvia Herrera Delgado
*Prayer: "Our Final Surrender"*
**9**

Blessed Are the Meek for They Shall Inherit the Earth /
Val Twanmoh
Artwork / Jose Enrique Portillo Delgado
*Prayer: "The Gift God Alone Can Give"*
**17**

## Blessed Are the Refugees

Blessed Are They Who Hunger and Thirst for Righteousness
for They Shall Be Satisfied /
Mikhael H. Borgonos
Artwork / Ana Silvia Herrera Delgado
*Prayer: "In the Right with God"*
27


Blessed Are the Merciful for They Shall Receive Mercy /
Cary Plamondon
Artwork / Jose Enrique Portillo Delgado
*Prayer: "How Eyes of Mercy See the World"*
35


Blessed Are the Pure of Heart for They Shall See God /
Andrea Naft
Artwork / Jose Enrique Portillo Delgado
*Prayer: "The Depth from Which All Else Springs"*
45


Blessed Are the Peacemakers for They Shall Be Called
Children of God / Andrea Naft
Artwork / Jose Enrique Portillo Delgado
*Prayer: "The True Daughters and Sons of God"*
55

# Contents

Blessed Are They Who Are Persecuted for the Sake
of Righteousness, for Theirs Is the Kingdom of Heaven /
Scott Rose
Artwork / Ana Silvia Herrera Delgado
*Prayer: "Witnesses Worthy of the Kingdom"*
**63**


Rejoice and Be Glad / Scott Rose
Artwork / Jose Enrique Portillo Delgado
*Prayer: "Blessed Are the Refugees, for They Are
the Presence of God"*
77


About the Organizations     **87**
About the Artists     **88**
About the Authors     **89**

*Foreword*

This small book has a large heart.

In it you are going to hear the stories of young immigrant children who have fled violence in Central America and prevailed over often harrowing hardship. Their stories are unique and powerful, but also far too common in our world today.

In my dealings with leaders in Central America, I found yet again how important personal contact and commitment to building relationships are not only for understanding people but also for creative politics. While others have said that "all politics is local," I have long held the view that "all politics is personal." The longer you know someone, the greater the possibility of trust. And with trust we gain greater understanding, better cooperation, and more peaceful outcomes.

We continue to live in a world with more refugees and displaced people than at any time since World War II. We are being challenged as countries, as policymakers, and most importantly, as human beings. We need voices like Father O'Donovan, Scott Rose, and their coauthors who remind us of our common humanity—and our obligations to one another. Sometimes that can be uncomfortable because so often we fall short.

I've had the privilege of knowing Father O'Donovan for many years. Over that time, he has provided great wisdom and solace to my family and me. And I will be forever grateful for his presence and his kind words at the service for my son Beau.

With this book, I hope many others will gain the benefit of Father O'Donovan's wisdom and that of his coauthors, and that readers' hearts will be enlarged by encountering the children in these stories.

*Joe Biden*

# Is God Watching?

Let me begin with two images most of us have seen in the media.

Several years ago, the dead body of a little boy washed up on the shore of the Mediterranean and brought heartbreakingly home to the world the cost of one family's effort to flee the civil war in Syria. We could not take our aching eyes off the body of little Alan Kurdi.

About a year later, another child, Omran Daqneesh, lanced what was left of our hearts. We saw him in the rubbish of the historic city of Aleppo, after a Russian airstrike, sitting on an orange ambulance chair, covered in ashes like a little ghost. Later, according to his father, he became a political pawn.

The plight of refugees and displaced persons is not the only crisis besetting humanity in today's world. The delicate ecological balance of what Pope Francis calls "our common home" is, according to overwhelming scientific evidence, seriously endangered. The threat of misused nuclear power has become alarmingly greater, with nuclear arms now in the possession of more states and the efforts to curtail them stalled by what seems a modern fatalism. The increasing gulf between rich and poor throughout the world—even granting the large numbers of people who have in the past century been raised from poverty—threatens not only the human rights and dignity of the poor but the stability of nations and the world order itself.

But the great number of refugees and internally displaced persons today is no less a threat to our very humanity. According to the United Nations High Commissioner on Refugees (UNHCR), by the end of 2016 there were 65.6 million people forcibly displaced worldwide, an increase of 300,000 over the previous year. (To imagine this concretely: it is roughly the number of people in all of Britain.) Of the 65.6 million displaced: 22.5 million were refugees in the technical sense (driven out of their countries by fear of persecution); 40.3 million were internally displaced (still within their home countries but likewise driven from their homes, schools, and communities); and 2.8 million were asylum seekers. Children below the age of 18 are now over half of the refugee population. "The number of new displacements," says the UNHCR, "was equivalent to 20 people being forced to flee their homes every minute of 2016."

Misconceptions abound. It is not the *developed* world that is hosting the greatest number of refugees but the *developing* world (which in fact can least afford it). Syria is not the only source of refugees; they come also, in significant numbers, from Afghanistan, many regions of Africa, Central America (especially the Northern Triangle of El Salvador, Guatemala, and Honduras), and, most recently, Venezuela. Most refugees are not to be found in camps (30 percent), but in urban areas (the other 70 percent). And the average length of stay in a camp is not the "several months or years" most Westerners suppose—but a full seventeen years.

However robust your conception of God's providence, this situation threatens it deeply. You think of an early scene in Alice McDermott's novel *The Ninth Hour*, in which an awful act of self-destruction is about to occur and an elderly nun senses that God, bent over, must be holding his head between his hands, helpless.

Is God watching? Are we?

Is Jesus, God's incarnate word for us, watching?

The revered philosopher-theologian and spiritual guide Michael J. Buckley, S.J., likes to say that the gaze of Jesus, Jesus watching us, is "the first event of discipleship." And in January 2018, celebrating a Mass for peace and justice in Santiago, Chile, Pope Francis dwelt on the first words of chapter 5 in Matthew's Gospel: "When Jesus saw the crowd . . ." The Pope suggested that in the gaze of Jesus the people encountered "the echo of their longings and aspirations." That encounter gave rise to the Beatitudes, "born of the compassionate heart of Jesus" and a horizon toward which we are all called still today. In proclaiming the Beatitudes, the Pope continued, Jesus "shakes us out of that negativity, that sense of resignation that makes us think we can have a better life if we escape from our problems, shun others, hide within our comfortable existence, dulling our senses with consumerism." Such a "sense of resignation," he warned, "tends to isolate us from others, to divide and separate us, to blind us to life around us and to the suffering of others." Put positively, the Pope was calling us to solidarity with our fellow human beings, and especially with the poor and those in greatest need.

Solidarity has become an increasingly insistent theme of Catholic social teachings at least since Pope Saint John Paul II. It has been proposed along two converging lines of thought, one explicitly religious and the other from the practical wisdom of common human reflection.

Religiously, the witness of Scripture has a paramount authority, and especially Hebrew Scripture is insistent on the people's duties toward strangers and aliens. The two defining moments in the history of the Jewish people—the Exodus and the Exile—led to powerful theologies of liberation, one testifying to God's deliverance of the people from enforced labor in Egypt and toward a promised land, and the other lamenting enforced displacement in Babylon but celebrating the people's return to the land of the promise. Recalling the Exodus, Yahweh repeatedly commands the people to love the stranger and the alien, for they too had been strangers in a foreign land (Deut 10:19; Exod 23:9; Lev 19:33-34). As a providentially delivered people, they are called to loving hospitality, not merely as a social nicety but as a sacred necessity, mimicking the protective care of their Lord. "The alien who resides with you shall be to you as the citizen among you; you shall love the alien as yourself, for you were aliens in the land of Egypt: I am the LORD your God" (Lev 19:34).

In more recent history, a watershed moment came in the aftermath of World War II, the last time the world saw anything approaching the current refugee crisis. Meeting in San Francisco to establish the United Nations, world leaders were able to adopt the landmark *Universal Declaration of Human Rights* (1948). Later the *Convention Related to the Status of Refugees* was adopted

(1951). Both were supported by argument that was, if variously influenced by religious themes, nevertheless basically grounded in purely rational terms.

Today, of course, the question of refugees and people on the move is a matter of significant controversy in American society. Imagined threats are often trumpeted far beyond what reliable evidence supports. And the riches that migrants bring to our country are all too easily overlooked. Here voices such as Senator George Mitchell's are important to hear: "Three of the most valuable and successful business enterprises in the world are Apple, Amazon, and Google. Apple was created by Steve Jobs, whose father was born in Syria. Amazon was created by Jeff Bezos, whose adoptive father was born in Cuba. And a cofounder of Google was Sergey Brin, who was born in Russia." We may also note that of the seven Americans who won Nobel Prizes in 2016, six are immigrants (winning in chemistry, physics, and economics).

Calling for a conversion of mind and heart vis-à-vis migrants that is both religiously and rationally grounded, the bishops of the United States and Mexico in 2003 authored a still valuable document titled "Strangers No Longer: Together on the Journey of Hope." The conversion called for, they wrote, "deals with confronting attitudes of cultural superiority, indifference and racism; accepting migrants not as foreboding aliens, terrorists or economic threats, but as persons with dignity and rights, revealing the presence of Christ; and recognizing migrants as bearers of deep cultural values and rich faith traditions."

*Blessed Are the Refugees* is offered as a humble resource, through stories and images and prayers, to support such conversion of mind and heart. We hope it will help readers to see, as God calls us to see, what is achingly happening in God's world—and then, fired with God's love, to join the Holy Spirit in seeking to renew the earth.

—*Leo J. O'Donovan, S.J.*

# Introduction

For the past several years, in my role as a permanent deacon in the Catholic Church, I have had the great honor to provide volunteer legal services at the Esperanza Center, a program of Catholic Charities of Baltimore that provides healthcare, education, and immigration legal assistance to thousands of undocumented people. In this work, I have been especially moved by the suffering and strength of children served by Esperanza who have fled from Central America without their families to escape violence.

*Blessed Are the Refugees* compiles stories and spiritual reflections about these youth, written by Esperanza employees and volunteers, with each child's story shared in the context of a Beatitude. Artwork was created by a refugee youth served by Esperanza who lives in Maryland and by her teenage brother who lives in El Salvador.

Each chapter includes a meditative prayer written by Father Leo J. O'Donovan, S.J., Director of Mission for Jesuit Refugee Service/USA, another important Catholic organization that provides health, education, and social services to refugees, including chaplaincy care to many of Esperanza's children when they were first held in detention centers on the border before being placed temporarily with relatives in Maryland, pending deportation proceedings.

The book's authors and artists have instructed that all royalties from sales of *Blessed Are the Refugees* be directed to the Esperanza Center and Jesuit Refugee Service in support of these organizations.

According to the U.S. Customs and Border Protection, in fiscal years 2014 through 2016, over 168,000 children migrated alone to the United States and were detained at the southern border. While this dramatic trend has slowed down, the youth still come—to escape suffering that is difficult for most Americans to even imagine. Gang violence, extreme poverty, and lack of government protective services for children place them in extraordinary vulnerability and pain.

The depth of that suffering is evident in the very fact that the children flee alone. Most youth in the world choose to remain among family and friends despite poverty and abuse. One can imagine how terrible the situation must be for children to be driven to flee, embarking alone on what they know will be a long, dangerous, and traumatizing journey to the United States. One Esperanza child was raped on the way. Another was kidnapped at gunpoint. It only takes talking to a few of the youth to understand the truth about a great myth: these children aren't *running toward the American dream*; they're *running away from personal nightmare*. The point at which they flee is when the trauma of staying becomes greater than the trauma of leaving. That point for Alberto was when his father's twice-weekly beatings escalated from belts to the flat edge of a machete. That's when Alberto fled. For his sister, Roberta, that point was a year later, when the father turned the machete around and threatened to kill her with the sharp edge. For Luisa, that crisis point came when she witnessed the gang murder of her cousin, and the killers knew that she saw it. She fled the next day.

*Blessed Are the Refugees* uses various terms to describe the children, including "refugee," "immigrant youth," and the more specific reference, "unaccompanied children" (because they migrated without a parent or legal guardian). Some children may not meet the precise legal definition of refugee that refers to people who flee their home to another country in order to escape persecution for specific reasons such as race or social group. The special circumstance of these children, however, is not adequately captured by the more general term "immigrant," which encompasses all noncitizens, including refugees, who intend to reside in the United States, some of whom do not have legal status for that residency. "Immigrant" implies a person who *chooses* to resettle to another country in order to *improve the future prospects for themselves and their families.* In contrast, a refugee is *driven* here in order *to survive.* The children in this book who flee Central America alone to escape violence are more like refugees. Indeed, in some ways, the federal government treats them as such by initially placing them in the custody of the U.S. Office of Refugee Resettlement after they are detained at the border.

On the other hand, while the authors seek to educate readers not in the immigration field about the vulnerability and suffering of these children, we also strive to convey their strength, ability, and dignity. While they were *forced* to flee, they had the *strength to flee*—alone, with full knowledge of the dangerousness of the trip and the struggle of living undocumented in a foreign country. Even more impressive are the skill and grace with which they overcome obstacles that might paralyze the average American teenager who has not been challenged by tragedy. Most remarkable is how the children contribute in significant ways to their families, friends, and communities in the United States.

The authors also seek to share personal ways in which the children have touched our lives. This is intended to further emphasize the capability of these children to teach and inspire, and, for readers who serve in the immigration field, we hope to reignite their passion. It is not intended to shift the focus away from the children, nor to suggest that the challenges of our service in any way match the pain and struggle of the children. On the contrary, we hope to convey that not only do we cherish the divine within the children we serve, but that we have been blessed to learn from them and grow because of them.

Some Americans are hesitant about helping these children because they think we don't have the resources to take care of them. The Esperanza staff understand, firsthand, the challenge of overwhelming need. There are many times when they, like the innkeeper to the journeying Holy Family, might want to say there is no room. But the staff keep their arms open, focus on one child at a time, and find inspiration in the Gospel story in which Jesus multiplies five loaves and two fish to feed five thousand people. This story of abundance flowing from love reminds us that when we are faced with overwhelming need, God calls us to pray—first to discern the most loving response and then for the energy and creativity to act. Otherwise, we make decisions out of fear, not love, and our responses are more limited. Coincidentally, in 2015 and 2016, approximately five thousand refugee children from Central America were temporarily placed in Maryland to await deportation proceedings. I believe that Jesus is blessing the small band of Esperanza employees, just as he blessed the five loaves and two fish, to meet that great need. Indeed, the multiplication of resources continues each month, with over five hundred volunteers now, including one hundred pro bono attorneys.

As recorded at the end of Matthew's Gospel, the risen Jesus tells his disciples to return to Galilee to meet him (Matt 28:16). There he instructs them to "make disciples of all nations." While this command is a call to evangelize, in the context of this book it can be heard as including our responsibility to care for immigrant youth from all areas of the world. And this responsibility brings with it great reward. As communities in the United States care for these children, the youth give back to those communities, inspiring people with their resilience, purity, humility, and faith.

## Blessed Are the Refugees

At Esperanza Center and Jesuit Refugee Service, we are honored to accompany these children for a short part of their journey and to have our lives touched—and changed—by theirs.

*Scott Rose*

## Where True Happiness Can Be Found

*Call us around you, Lord Jesus.*
*Let us sit near to you and hear*
*what the kingdom of the gospel is like.*
*Tell us where our true happiness can be found,*
*how we are blessed by your Father even when we least imagine it.*
*Help us not to seek cheap comfort and consolation.*
*We seek what you will teach, what you will touch,*
*what you will take with you.*

*We have heard how you were baptized by John at the Jordan*
*and how in synagogues throughout Galilee*
*you preached repentance for the coming kingdom of heaven.*
*You called simple people to follow after you.*
*You proclaimed good news of God's presence,*
*teaching all who would listen,*
*healing whoever came to you.*

*We must be here with you now.*
*What will you tell us?*
*We tremble with expectation.*
*Hope breaks out from our hearts to hear what you might say.*
*Gather us around you, Lord.*
*Tell us what it means to be blessed.*

—Leo J. O'Donovan, S.J.

# BLESSED ARE THE REFUGEES

BLESSED ARE THE POOR IN SPIRIT

# Blessed Are the Poor in Spirit for Theirs Is the Kingdom of Heaven

*Scott Rose*

Commentators on the Sermon on the Mount in Matthew and the Sermon on the Plain in Luke note the difference between this Beatitude's version in the two Gospels. Luke focuses solely on the physical suffering and social status of "the poor," while Matthew adds the spiritual dimension of the "poor in spirit," implying that physical deprivation can lead to a greater dependence on God. In both versions, though, Jesus is talking about people who live in physical poverty. The Greek word *ptochoi* used by Matthew in this Beatitude to describe the poor means people who are without basic physical necessities. The corresponding Hebrew word, *anawim*, implies oppression and humiliation. In Matthew's Beatitude, the "poor in spirit" are people who are physically poor and spiritually *humble.*

Maria was both.

She grew up so *poor* that she always went to sleep hungry, with only one, maybe two, meals each day. She only had one pair of shoes. The house she lived in was so small she had to share a bedroom with her grandparents. She became sick often but was never given medical care.

Even more challenging, she was *humbled* by abuse, oppressed and humiliated as implied by the Hebrew *anawim*. Her father abandoned her when she was four years old. Her mother physically abused her from age four to age eight, almost every day, hitting her in the face with a fist, so hard that Maria's mouth bled. The mother then abandoned Maria when she was eight, leaving her with the maternal grandparents and a twenty-year-old male cousin, all three of whom proceeded to abuse the child. For almost a year, until Maria was nine, the cousin raped her three times a week in a barn near the house.

Then, from ages nine to sixteen, Maria was physically abused at least weekly by the grandmother, and from ages fourteen to sixteen, she was sexually molested by the grandfather weekly. She fled from the house at age sixteen after he threatened to rape her. She moved around several times until she was twenty when she finally fled from El Salvador and took the dangerous trip alone to the United States to seek safety.

Unfortunately, the journey was traumatic as well. She was sexually harassed and assaulted many times. She walked in the desert for three days without food or water. Each day, she trudged from late afternoon to early morning, except for the last twenty-four hours during which she had no breaks at all. Out of desperation one day, she drank water from a cattle trough—a parallel to the poverty and humility of the Christ Child. Jesus rested in a manger. Maria drank from one. She became extremely ill because the water was contaminated.

She made her way to the East Coast in search of relatives who might help her. A testament to the goodness and loyalty of the vast majority of Central American families, Maria's cousins in Maryland welcomed her into their homes and cared for her with great love and generosity. Her father, who had abandoned her when she was so young and had later migrated to Virginia, invited her to visit him from time to time in order to reconcile.

Child abuse occurs everywhere, including the United States. The unique challenges faced by these immigrant children lie in the inability of law enforcement to protect them from domestic abuse and neglect when it occurs, and from gang violence that is continual and pervasive. This danger exacerbates the poverty and creates ongoing trauma.

As with many of the children served by Esperanza, Maria's resilience and faith are inspiring. The fact that she survived poverty and abuse is a testament to her inner resolve. The fact that she became a kind and hopeful young woman speaks of her grace-filled spirit. What touched me most—and changed me—were her wisdom and spiritual detachment from materialism, a poverty of spirit that was born from physical poverty.

When my parish was faced with the moral dilemma about how much money to spend on the construction of a new church building as opposed to outreach to the poor, I asked Maria her thoughts on the issue. Should we buy bricks or bread? I was surprised with her counterintuitive reply and the nuance of insight. She said that of course a church must help to alleviate poverty, but she was emphatic that sufficient money should be spent to make the building beautiful. She went on to share with me the basis of her view. Evidently, her respite during her traumatic childhood was her Catholic church in El Salvador, the only place she felt safe. And this building got her through her darkest moments. During these traumatic experiences, she would deal with the pain by dissociating (as trauma victims often do) and would imagine herself kneeling alone in front of the beautiful altar in that building.

I'm sure that the loving people of the parish were a significant reason for her fond memories. But she said that the image that got her through her pain—and prevented her from killing herself—was the building, not the people. Her physical poverty and abuse catalyzed, not thwarted, spiritual humility and insight that transcended my categorical, either-or thinking. For Maria, it didn't come down to a choice between bricks or bread. For her, bricks can nurture, too—just like bread.

When I imagine that grace-filled child kneeling before the altar in the Salvadoran church, I believe even more in the miracle of love, like bread becoming the Body of Christ. But when I think of that brave girl steeling herself with faith while being violated, I am inspired with greater insight about the boundless, transformative power of God—like bricks becoming bread.

Part of the legal process to obtain a green card for abused migrant children includes a state court hearing in which the child and his or her guardian seek to prove the past abuse, neglect, or abandonment and why it is in the best interests of the child to remain in the United States. In Maria's case, as noted above, her cousin who lived in Maryland was willing to be her guardian. When Maria and I were preparing for her hearing, I asked her to talk about her life in Maryland. She used the word "heaven" to describe the United States as compared to El Salvador. That term surprised me because I knew that she still struggled here. Frequent nightmares demonstrated that her unresolved trauma still haunted her. She couldn't work because she wasn't authorized to. She didn't speak any English, so she felt lost most of the time. While her cousin and his family were very kind to her, they were still strangers, so she felt very alone.

I realized that while this life is not what I would consider to be heaven, it is not the hell from which she had fled. Maria's faith was too simple to wrestle with the theology of Jesus's reference to the kingdom of heaven that, he says, belongs to the poor in spirit. And she is too humble to expect to be part of any kingdom. She just wants safety, three meals a day, and an altar she can kneel in front of every now and then.

## Simple Trust in God

*Lord, we hear you again telling us*
*that it is a blessing, happiness,*
*God's celebration of God's hope for us,*
*when we are poor.*

*The poor, and above all whoever is poor in spirit,*
*whoever has little or nothing but confidence in God,*
*you begin by teaching us, Lord,*
*they are blessed, happy, fortunate before your Father.*

*It is not, Lord, what we expect to hear.*
*The people of Israel thought poverty was a misfortune.*
*And when we today look around us*
*and see the dispossessed fellow human beings who are poor—*
*without any material resources,*
*in the most material meaning of the word—*
*we instinctively ask:*
*Are they happy?*
*Can their unreserved trust in God—"in spirit"—*
*be the source of real happiness?*
*Can an abused young girl like Maria really be happy?*
*Who believes that in the world around us?*

*And yet it is exactly what you say, preach, teach, and proclaim.*

## Blessed Are the Refugees

*Here on this imagined mount where God meets God's people,*
*you tell us—comfort us, challenge us, call us—*
*to believe that simply to have trust in God is beatitude indeed.*

*For the reign of God,*
*the realm of God's kingdom,*
*is where God first cares for the poor.*
*As God is caring now for Maria.*

—Leo J. O'Donovan, S.J.

# Blessed Are They Who Mourn for They Shall Be Comforted

*Andrea Naft*

As a teacher and parent, I witness children grow into their potential. Lives have beginnings and middles, but completeness comes with death. When a person dies, we can see who they became, and take meaning and comfort from the person's life. Each time I have lost a loved one, friend, or acquaintance, I experience how mourning and grief eventually bring spiritual comfort. So it was with Adan, a young man I met while volunteering as a Spanish interpreter for Esperanza Center.

In my Jewish tradition, the mourners' prayer, the Kaddish, does not mention the dead. It praises God. For a close relative, the mourner recites it daily for eleven months. This good deed brings merit to the relative in the "World to Come" and comfort and a closeness to our loved ones and God.

The depth of sadness intended in this Beatitude is conveyed by the use of the word *pentheo*, the Greek word for mourn that implies the extreme grief of death

BLESSED ARE THE REFUGEES

BLESSED ARE THEY WHO MOURN

or significant loss. This Beatitude (as well as others) is linked to Hebrew Scriptures in Isaiah 61:1-3:

> The spirit of the Lord GOD is upon me,
> because the LORD has anointed me;
> he has sent me to bring good news to the oppressed,
> to bind up the brokenhearted,
> to proclaim liberty to the captives,
> and release to the prisoners;
> to proclaim the year of the LORD's favor,
> and the day of vengeance of our God;
> to comfort all who mourn;
> to provide for those who mourn in Zion—
> to give them a garland instead of ashes,
> the oil of gladness instead of mourning,
> the mantle of praise instead of a faint spirit.

Recalling in some ways the struggle of undocumented immigrants in the United States, the Isaiah passage conveys the collective sadness of Israel during its Babylonian exile.

Adan was a person of extraordinary deeds and love, delivered in humble and ordinary ways. I have photos of him, but the flash of a camera could not capture his quiet greatness, depth of feeling, and loving heart. Nor could it reveal how he helped his family flee danger in their homeland. Nowhere in the photos can one see that he sacrificed his youth and education to support others. He would never have thought himself a hero, but he was.

We first met over a pizza in a restaurant. I was to interpret for Scott, a coauthor of this book, who was preparing for a hearing for Adan's younger brother, Williams. Adan was magnetic and joyful, glad to be helping his high school-aged brother. Since arriving in the United States ten years before, Adan supported himself and siblings as a cook, saving precisely to bring his brother and sister to safety in the United States.

Adan fled El Salvador due to domestic violence and poverty when he was eighteen. His father had been forced to fight in a brutal war civil war when he was only a teenager. Plagued with post-traumatic stress disorder (PTSD), the father drank and took out his frustrations violently on his children. So Adan fled by making the arduous journey on foot and by bus to the United States and then on to Maryland where he created a new life to help the siblings he left behind join him.

His brother followed ten years later at age fourteen. Adan physically and emotionally supported his little brother in every way possible. When they first met with Scott, both of these strong boys broke down and cried as they shared their history. They grieved the challenges life brought them without complaint or blame of others. They both cried again at Williams's hearing. They held the courage and strength within to create their own futures. Adan devoted all his time and youth to supporting the family.

His giving, brave attitude brought great comfort to those around him. Sadly, Adan's heavy work schedule kept him from learning English, attending college, and having a girlfriend. Yet Adan grieved even the loss of his young adulthood with acceptance. He rejoiced that his younger brother had a better life than he.

Williams became a star for Esperanza because of his willingness to share his tragic story publicly. That story exemplified the terrible circumstances that force children to flee from Central America, taking the dangerous trip alone to the United States. He was featured in television news stories and newspaper articles. Adan was proud of the attention and praise given to Williams. Behind the scenes, Adan quietly supported the cause of immigration reform in Maryland, driving Williams wherever he needed to go to help and encouraging Williams to continue the work.

The year passed. Adan continued to support his family, including the addition of his fifteen-year-old nephew who fled El Salvador. A sweetheart entered Adan's life and became his fiancée.

The last time I saw Adan he was twenty-eight years old. He leaned into my car's open window. With bright eyes and a warm smile, he thanked me in Spanish for taking Williams to a ceremony ordaining Scott as a permanent deacon in the Catholic Church. Williams was given the honor of doing one of the readings for the service, and I was helping him practice his English. Adan could not get the day off work. He sacrificed participation in the special event to work the job he was so grateful to have. In awe of Adan's maturity, I wished that I, in my mid-sixties, could meet life with such grace.

Two months later, Scott phoned me with a grief-heavy voice. Adan had taken his family and fiancée for a vacation to the ocean. When his nephew was swept out in the undertow, Adan swam out to him. He pulled and pushed the child toward safety, but Adan, not good at swimming and exhausted, could not make it back. He waved goodbye to his loved ones on shore and was gone. He lost his life the way he lived it: sacrificing himself for others and accepting with grace the suffering life brought him.

I understand that Adan's family and fiancée are still mourning. Like Adan, they do so without complaint or blame, their acceptance freeing the nephew from guilt so that he does not need to suffer more than he already does, grieving the loss of his family and friends back in El Salvador.

I too mourn the loss of Adan's life. His spirit, deeds, and love inspire my actions. My wish to help others increases. I praise God, thankful to be on this earth and grateful for the honor to share a small part of this family's journey.

## Our Final Surrender

*Why is it a blessing to mourn, Lord?*
*What happiness is there in the dark emptiness that enfolds us*
*when someone we deeply love departs this life?*
*Who can ever replace a lost spouse, a friend from our youth,*
*an innocent child?*
*Even the fact that at our birth we are already dying*
*has unnerved us poor mortals from the very beginning.*

*Is the blessing perhaps that whoever is mourning*
*is joining you in your grief over the city of Jerusalem,*
*or your tears for your friend Lazarus?*
*Is it a blessing to mourn because you too mourned?*
*As did your own mother at your death,*
*and your closest friends as well,*
*Mary Magdalene, the disciples on their way to Emmaus,*
*indeed, the saints of all the centuries.*

*Or perhaps it is a blessing to mourn*
*because the grief that follows death is the unfolding time*
*that reveals death for what it really is,*
*or at least can be:*
*our final surrender to your Father*
*of what our Father too has first given us to cherish and care for:*
*our lives as God's image.*

# BLESSED ARE THE REFUGEES

*Perhaps we cannot give our lives, or the lives of those we love,*
*back to God our Father except in a moment*
*that also extends over time.*

*Gracious Lord, show us your Father mourning with us,*
*knowing the cost, the pain, the mystery of life*
*redeemed through time*
*in your Holy Spirit.*
*Then indeed we shall be comforted.*

—Leo J. O'Donovan, S.J.

# Blessed Are the Meek
# for They Shall Inherit the Earth
*Val Twanmoh*

The first thing that struck me when I met Sofia was the sense of warmth and calm she carried with her and the obvious love and sense of responsibility that she felt for Gabriela, her younger sister. The way they told their stories to me with quiet strength and humble resolve belied the nightmare that pushed Gabriela to leave her home in Honduras and make the dangerous journey north to reunite with Sofia in Baltimore. It struck me then that, despite their outward appearance as two young women who were meek, they were far from being weak.

In my role as director of the Esperanza Center, I don't often have the opportunity to provide direct service to our immigrant clients. When our legal services team asked if I would help provide representation for one of the unaccompanied children who needed counsel, I was pleased to reengage the twenty years of legal practice that I had previously "retired," and so I

BLESSED ARE THE REFUGEES

BLESSED ARE THE MEEK

represented Sofia and Gabriela in the state court proceedings seeking to have Sofia appointed the legal guardian for Gabriela—the first step in Gabriela's quest for a green card that would allow her to stay in the United States under her sister's care.

In Honduras, Sofia and Gabriela lived with their mother, two brothers, and Sofia's two daughters in a small two-bedroom house made of cement blocks. As the oldest of the four, in a household with no father and a mother who was too old to obtain work in Honduras, Sofia provided most of the income for the family from her work in a clothing factory, but it was barely enough for the family to survive. At the age of twenty-five, she left for the United States to find better work to support the family. She found a job in a restaurant in Baltimore and was able to send money home to help pay for school for the children and put food on their table. A year later, her oldest brother left to find work, and shortly thereafter the younger brother and Sofia's oldest daughter followed.

With no men left in the household, Gabriela, her mother, and her cousin became targets for the gangs in their town. Gang members would come and, when they found Gabriela or her cousin, they would beat them with machetes. Gabriela and her cousin have scars from the cuts left by the machete swords. Her mother would report the beatings to the police, but nothing was done.

The beatings and terrorizing of Gabriela's family continued for over five years.

In the spring of 2013, when she was fourteen years old, Gabriela, fearful of the gangs and the lack of any police protection, left home to make the journey to the United States to reunite with her siblings. It took her four days to get from Honduras to the U.S. border, traveling mostly by car and bus, relying on strangers for food and a place to rest. She survived on three potatoes a day, and one day she was able to get some chicken to eat. After two days of traveling through Honduras and Guatemala, she crossed part of Mexico and made it to a small, dirty bodega, the equivalent of a pantry/shelter for people. She was one of only two females with over a dozen men crammed into the bodega, which was overrun with mice and roaches. Frightened and hungry, she got little sleep, and then spent the fourth day continuing the journey to the United States. When she crossed the border, scared and alone, she was apprehended by immigration officials and detained in a shelter for eighteen days in California. She was then released into the care of her older sister, Sofia, in Baltimore, and the two siblings sought assistance and counsel at the Esperanza Center.

To me, Sofia and Gabriela, as with many of our immigrant clients, exemplify the Beatitude "Blessed are the meek," but not in the way one might expect.

There has been much commentary regarding traditional and contemporary interpretations of this Beatitude centering around the meaning of the term "meek" and whether it was intended to connote a submissive, resigned, weak attribute (a more contemporary usage that would raise questions about why such character would be rewarded) or whether it must be taken in a more biblical framework. For me, the most appropriate meaning and likely intention of the use of the word by Jesus, a refugee and immigrant himself, is not a weak submissiveness to fate, as biblical scholar Samuel A. Meier states, but rather a "patient and hopeful endurance of undesirable circumstances" that identifies the person as "externally vulnerable and weak but inwardly resilient and strong." Meekness does not identify the weak, Meier says, but more precisely the strong who have been placed in a position of weakness where they persevere without giving up.

It's that inner strength of Sofia and Gabriela that fills me with such admiration, respect, and awe, and the seemingly odd combination with such humility. Equally impressive were the outward determination of both women and the substantial contributions they have made to their families and communities.

Despite the challenges she faced, and the fear and threats to her physical and emotional well-being that she had to endure, Gabriela has not only survived; she has succeeded. She graduated from high school with very good grades—a significant accomplishment for a girl who began with no proficiency in English. She secured a part-time job as a hostess in a restaurant, where she is able to set aside her normally shy tendencies and greet people with confidence and pride, welcoming customers just as she was welcomed to the United States. She juggles that with attending college in Baltimore, with the career goal of becoming an immigration attorney, so that she can help others just as she and her sister were helped in their time of need. How fitting of her unique attributes that she chose a field that requires assertiveness and yet also needs humility. Her community now—and the thousands of people she will serve as an attorney in the future—are fortunate that she has become a permanent legal resident, and in several years will become a citizen of the United States.

Sofia's inspiring strength also contributes to her family and her community. When she was assaulted, she contacted the police and assisted in the successful prosecution of the perpetrator. She now offers assistance to other women who find themselves victims of violence. Like Gabriela, her unique combination of humility and strength demonstrates the true meaning of meekness. She never expected the United States to give her special treatment. She always believed it was her responsibility to earn what she needed for herself and her family.

And yet, she also believes that she needs to give back to her community. That responsibility included taking personal risk to ensure the safety of her family and community by helping the government prosecute a violent offender, thus risking retribution by that perpetrator and deportation because she was an undocumented individual. Her unique strength allowed her to fulfill her responsibility, proving again that she was far more than a victim to life's challenges.

If you were to meet Sofia and Gabriela on the street, you would see a girl and her motherly older sister, seemingly quiet and self-composed, shy, and unassuming. You might guess that they would not speak up for themselves, challenge any authority, or seek more than what may be offered. You might see a teenager completing her schooling, improving her English, and playing soccer with friends, and her older sister working six days a week to provide for her siblings and her children in the hope of a better life. But you would be missing the strength, the resolve, the courage, and the faith in God and in each other that brought the two girls to the new land, a new culture, a new beginning—the earth they will inherit.

## The Gift God Alone Can Give

*"Meek," Lord?*
*Should we really be meek?*
*It's not a word often used today in praise of someone.*
*But then we often don't know who really to praise.*
*We're here with you to learn who should be praised,*
*and why*
*and the difference it makes.*

*If we knew the Psalms as well as many of your disciples*
*and the crowd who first gathered around you,*
*we would know what courage and resolve accompanied*
*this word for your people Israel.*
*They knew the threat of foreign kingdoms*
*encroaching on them.*
*They knew the rampant injustice that surrounded them.*
*They knew above all the infidelity of their own hearts.*

*But they knew also the blessing of patience,*
*confident waiting*
*for the retribution the Holy One alone could bring.*
*They had heard the psalmist sing of being still*
*before the Lord,*
*being slow to anger, being gentle toward others,*
*knowing that the Lord alone judges truly and finally.*

*Being slow to anger is not weakness, but can be called meek.*
*For what in fact can we finally possess,*
*what of the earth is really ours,*
*except the gift you alone can give?*
*Our true selves in our true home*
*in your true community of the just.*

—Leo J. O'Donovan, S.J.

# BLESSED ARE THE REFUGEES

BLESSED ARE THEY WHO HUNGER AND THIRST

# Blessed Are They Who Hunger and Thirst for Righteousness for They Shall Be Satisfied

*Mikhael H. Borgonos*

"I ran toward my house while [the MS-13 gang member] watched. I heard a very loud noise and felt something whiz by my head. He was shooting at me. He continued to shoot and one of the bullets hit my hand."

Camila, an unaccompanied child from El Salvador whom I represented, recounted this story before a U.S. asylum officer. To her dismay, the officer denied Camila's application for asylum and referred her to an immigration judge. Camila hungered for righteousness, and she wasn't finding it.

Camila and most children we serve at Esperanza Center have fled violent circumstances in Central America's "Northern Triangle." A choir of newspapers and reputable magazines agree that the Northern Triangle is among the most dangerous places in the world. There, gang violence—particularly by the MS-13 and

Calle 18—is rampant. MS-13 members use knives and machetes to eliminate rivals and anyone who gets in their way. Calle 18 and other gangs shoot to kill and display victims' bodies for all to see. Gruesome images of severed heads and dismembered bodies fill the nightly TV news. Rape and murder are gang initiation rites. Government services as basic as drafting police reports are no longer worth the effort of law enforcement and citizens.

Camila did not ask for help and protection from the Salvadoran police; she was afraid of the police because, according to her, the police acted with the gangs. Hungering for safety, children like Camila leave their neighborhoods in the dark of night and trek the long journey to the United States.

Before journeying to the United States from El Salvador, Camila suffered harassment by a member of the MS-13 gang in El Salvador who ultimately tried to kill her. During these confrontations, Camila learned something about the gang member that he did not want anyone to know. This sparked a reign of terror against Camila and her family. The gang member found out where Camila lived and even described to her, in detail, her family's daily routine. Worse, he pulled a knife against Camila's father and younger brother and threatened to kidnap them. Camila switched schools several times in El Salvador to avoid the gang member's reach, but he still found Camila and shot at her multiple times and nearly killed her. She survived.

Because it was too dangerous to live where they were, Camila's family sold their car and scraped money together for her land passage to the United States—a decision that she described as painful and heart-wrenching. She traveled through Guatemala and Mexico where police officers took her money and placed their hands around her body to look for anything valuable. In turn, and hungering for a crumb of safety and peace, Camila's family sold their home and moved in with family members elsewhere in El Salvador.

Unfortunately, for Camila and many children seeking refuge, the trauma does not stop once they enter the United States. Some children have few or no family roots, and the cycle of fear can begin anew because the same gangs that the children escaped in their home country also operate in the United States. Even more tragically, the U.S. government is sometimes not able to ensure justice. Children are not guaranteed assistance of counsel in immigration cases, thereby leaving victimized, unaccompanied youth defenseless against their deportation charges. Each year, the U.S. government physically removes hundreds of thousands of vulnerable individuals and returns them to the pit of gang mayhem in the Northern Triangle. It looked as if Camila would be treated in the same way. But Esperanza Center fought on the girl's behalf, preparing for the next step in her case when she would appear before an immigration judge.

The process of seeking safety can traumatize again a person seeking refuge. Camila has cried many times with me, beginning when we completed her asylum application through to her receipt of the heavy news that the asylum office denied her request. These traumatic experiences have caused her to numb out, staring blankly at times, no longer speaking as much during our meetings, and even declining an opportunity to apply for a lawful U.S. work permit that she initially had been excited to pursue. Her behavior reminds me of how people respond to fasting or starvation after several days: the hunger and thirst begin to dissipate as the body and mind draw inward to survive.

I know that numbing out is not the healthiest reaction to trauma, so I encouraged Camila several times to seek mental health counseling. But, like most undocumented youth in the United States, she never was able to break through all the emotional and financial barriers to follow through with counseling. I admire her tenacity in pursuing her case, and I accept that, sometimes, a person just needs to lower her head and get through the situation and keep moving forward.

What has inspired me most, though, is how this girl who hungered—physically, when she fled El Salvador, and emotionally, as she sought justice in the United States—has ended up feeding others.

A shy person by temperament, Camila secured a job selling items at a mall kiosk in order to help support her aunt, her young nephew, and herself. This personality stretch demonstrated her inner strength—the girl who in my office alternated between sobbing and numbing out is now an assertive saleswoman because that is what is needed to feed her family.

Camila juggles her job and high school with providing almost twenty hours per week of childcare for her young nephew while her aunt works. She also cooks often for her family, one of her favorite meals being pupusas, a traditional Salvadoran dish made of corn. In addition, Camila tends to her aging parents who reside in El Salvador, calling them frequently and sending money whenever she can.

I have learned from Camila that people who have hungered are the best equipped to nourish others, whether that be food or righteousness. Knowing the ache for both inspires empathy, promotes solidarity with the person in need, and directs action. I'm sure Camila, better than most American teenage babysitters, knows exactly when her young nephew is hungry and how best to respond. I'm equally sure that in her career she will be skilled in helping people at the right time in the most effective way.

Camila has even inspired me in the way I practice law. In part because of her patient, almost sacred persistence in seeking justice, I have chosen to follow a disappearing tradition in American jurisprudence that incorporates religious language in documents and oral presentation. Like some other attorneys, I still write the word "pray" in motions or verbal summaries before judges to ask courts to grant requests for justice and righteousness. We often refer to these court documents as "pleadings"—evidencing the longing that drives the prayer. I use that word now even more intentionally in Camila's pleadings, and I mean it with all the hunger in Camila's heart.

Camila's case is pending in immigration court, and it could take a few years before her trial occurs. The immigration court system is severely backlogged and needs at least a hundred more judges. While Camila waits, she works diligently to better herself, adjust to her new life in the United States, and help feed her family and community. I know that Camila will someday reap a sizeable harvest from her hard work, and I am certain she will share whatever she has with others who are in need.

## In the Right with God

*Lord Jesus, do we dare to dignify ourselves*
*as hungering and thirsting for righteousness?*

*When we read of the millions and millions*
*of refugees and migrants and displaced persons*
*in the world today—*
*and, Lord, we know that the heartbreaking majority*
*of them are children—*
*can we possibly claim that righteousness for them*
*is as important to us as food and water?*
*Don't we rather lower our eyes*
*and look almost desperately away?*

*What even do you mean by "righteousness"?*
*Committed people, generous people,*
*people of real engagement for the poor of the world*
*have long translated your word as "justice."*
*But we have been told that the people of Israel*
*did not have an abstract conception of justice*
*and its implications.*
*"Righteous" seems to have meant*
*someone who has been declared innocent,*
*someone "in the right" with God your Father.*

33

*Is God then the one who is really "righteous"?*
*Or is it what God does that defines "righteousness"?*
*But then surely your God will only declare "right"*
*those people in today's world who stand up,*
*"get right" for your children driven from their homes.*

*Help us, Jesus, to see those children of your Father.*
*Help us to see those sisters and brothers of yours.*
*Are they any less dear, precious, unique, irreplaceable*
*than any other of your—our—brothers and sisters?*

*Help us to see them, Lord.*
*Give us hunger and thirst that they be cared for.*
*Let us be not only poor in spirit,*
*aware of our mortality,*
*patient amid travail,*
*but also taught justice*
*by God's wonder-full acts of righteousness.*

—Leo J. O'Donovan, S.J.

# Blessed Are the Merciful
# for They Shall Receive Mercy
*Cary Plamondon*

In Greek and Roman cultures, showing mercy implied weakness rather than strength, to such an extent that the Greeks and Romans did not recognize mercy as a virtue. The concept of mercy hasn't gained much cultural traction over the years. We live in a time when revenge and seeking an eye for an eye is common, even expected. Seldom do we find expressions of mercy and merciful behavior in the media and much of daily life. Yet throughout his teachings and ultimately through his sacrifice on the cross, Jesus exemplified mercy and taught that in order to be in communion with God, we need to express mercy ourselves. How do we reconcile the world's view of getting back at those who have hurt us with a God who inspires us to be merciful?

In urging people to be witnesses to mercy, Pope John Paul II in his second encyclical, *Dives in misericordia* ("Rich in Mercy") (1980), noted that the "present-day mentality . . . seems opposed to a God of mercy, and in fact tends to exclude from life and to remove from the

# Blessed Are the Refugees

Blessed Are the Merciful

human heart the very idea of mercy."

Pope Francis emboldened us in his *Misericordiae Vultus: Bull of Indiction of the Extraordinary Jubilee of Mercy* (2015), stating, "[w]e are called to show mercy because mercy has first been shown to us. Pardoning offences becomes the clearest expression of merciful love, and for us Christians it is an imperative from which we cannot excuse ourselves." Pardoning offenses and showing mercy is a choice—most often a very difficult choice—that many of us think about but, more often than not, ultimately reject.

A teenager named Elena showed me that being merciful under difficult circumstances is a sign of strength, not weakness. She did that by choosing from a merciful heart to forgive her father who had abandoned and mistreated her.

Elena grew up in a small town in El Salvador. She often had little to eat and had a medical condition that required therapy to clear her lungs and also access to an inhaler. With no money for medicine or doctors, she was frequently hospitalized. When Elena was five, her father left El Salvador for the United States, ostensibly to find work and send money back to Elena and her mother so that Elena could get the medical help she needed. After several months, her father discontinued communication and sent no money for his daughter's care—in essence, abandoning his family. At the same time, Elena and her mother were threatened by men to whom Elena's father owed money.

Elena's mother felt the pain and desperation of trying to keep her daughter healthy and safe while having minimal access to medical resources and food. In search of a better life and access to medical care, Elena's mother with the now eight-year-old girl took the long and arduous journey to Texas to live with Elena's aunt. Elena's father, who lived in Baltimore, soon discovered that Elena was in the United States. Elena's delight at learning that her father was coming to see her was short-lived, as her father took her back to Baltimore to live with him, denying her mother access to Elena for a period of time.

Although Elena's father took care of the girl's medical needs and enrolled her in school, he also hit her when he became upset with her, and sometimes forced her to dress in boys' clothes, which humiliated her. Her health struggles were exacerbated because of this stress, and she had to be hospitalized many times.

Her father also controlled Elena's relationship with her mother, allowing only limited communication. As an eight-year-old, Elena didn't understand that her mother was trying to move closer to Elena or that her mother had no legal recourse to get Elena back, since her mother was undocumented. For four years, Elena believed the lies her father told her, and she grew bitter in her heart toward the mother she thought had loved her. In her naivete,

Elena didn't fully understand that her father was treating her in a controlling and abusive manner.

Eventually, Elena's mother moved to a small city in Maryland, never giving up hope that she would be reunited with her daughter. The father gave the mother limited access to her daughter, but Elena had mixed emotions about being with her mother. The girl blamed her mother for not fighting harder to get custody of her, and Elena felt they had become estranged over the years.

One December day when Elena was twelve, her father brought her to her mother's house and said he was going to El Salvador for a few weeks to see his mother but would return to get Elena. He never returned. About a year later, Elena read on Facebook that he had remarried and had a son with his new wife. He had provided no financial support to Elena and even requested financial help from her mother.

When I met Elena, she was sixteen and a dedicated student who spoke impeccable English. She first recounted her story to an intake attorney at Esperanza so that we could prepare her case in order for her to obtain her green card. She aimed to attend college and work one day in one of the medical professions, and so wanted to ensure that she was eligible for financial aid for further education.

As her attorney, I needed to know the facts of her case so that I could show the judge that Elena had been abused, neglected, or abandoned by her father, a prerequisite for the special type of green card she sought. Not surprisingly, Elena found it painful and sickening to discuss the facts of her initial and subsequent abandonment and the treatment she had received by her father when she lived with him. At the time, I didn't push Elena to open up, and we didn't speak about these specifics during the course of her case, but I was aware of them from her intake form.

At each of our meetings, Elena was accompanied by her mother, stepfather, and younger sister. It was heartwarming to see that Elena was loved, accepted, supported, and encouraged by a loving family. Elena and her mother had finally worked through the misunderstandings and pain of those confusing four years when Elena lived with her father and away from her mother.

Two years ago, I saw the pain and hurt in Elena's eyes when she thought about emotions relating to her father and their relationship. More recently, however, I have become reacquainted with Elena. She now speaks more regularly with her father on the phone and no longer harbors resentment toward him. As a result, she feels at peace. She explained that the years of instability and failing grades she experienced during middle school have spurred her to work harder and have given her a purpose that she may otherwise not have had.

It is, of course, always easier to show mercy and forgiveness to those who clearly love us back. The difficult task is giving those who have intentionally hurt us not what they may deserve but better than they deserve, as Pope Francis noted that we as Christians are called to do.

Dealing with serious relationship problems and then showing mercy to those people who contributed to her pain and hurt has made Elena stronger. By forgiving her father, Elena can focus now on the future and not allow the past to drag her down. The mercy she exhibits is inspiring, and it has allowed her to move forward on her life's path.

Elena's father returned to his home country and started another family, and Elena knows that she could choose to forgive her father or choose to abandon any relationship with him. Out of the strength she has gained in trusting God and letting go of her past hurt and pain, Elena chose to work on restoring the broken relationship with her father. I see in Elena's ability to forge a different relationship with a father who abandoned her not once, but twice, a reflection of God's mercy in restoring our broken relationship with God through Jesus.

Christ has been an essential part of Elena's journey of mercy, and I smiled knowingly and with gratitude when she told me she aims to pursue a career in a medical profession and was headed to a Pennsylvania university named *Mercyhurst.*

## How Eyes of Mercy See the World

*Gracious Lord, thank you for the Bishop of Rome*
*you have given us*
*and for his tireless preaching of mercy.*
*He seems to have taken all the attributes of God,*
*shaken them from the bag of learned thought and said to us,*
*"Look. See how they all shine more brightly*
*when you look at them with the eyes of mercy."*

*But you told us this in your great long sermon.*
*It is happiness, it is blessing, it is life fulfilled*
*if only we are merciful:*
*if we love our neighbor,*
*if we forgive our neighbor,*
*if we stop to care especially for our neighbor in need,*
*if we love even our enemies.*
*If the deepest movements of our hearts are not simply*
*for people close to us*
*but still more for people who seem distant, unusual*
*or strange.*
*As though we were not already strangers to ourselves!*

*A merciful heart recognizes in other hearts the needs,*
*the longings, the hurts, the healings*
*that make that heart whole in the very act of recognition.*

*Blessed Are the Merciful*

*How different the world looks, Lord,*
*when we look out at it mercifully.*
*There is much we may not understand;*
*but we will feel invited to understand.*
*There is much that may seem strange or puzzling;*
*but there we will discover paths for our own self-discovery.*
*There may even be much we are initially inclined to reject;*
*but the refusal of that rejection can prepare us*
*for the great risk of our own self-acceptance.*

*The eyes of mercy see the world as its merciful creator does:*
*good and true and beautiful,*
*to be loved and cherished,*
*forgiven and enfolded,*
*the partner infinitely and incomprehensibly beloved.*

—Leo J. O'Donovan, S.J.

# BLESSED ARE THE REFUGEES

BLESSED ARE THE PURE OF HEART

# Blessed Are the Pure of Heart for They Shall See God

*Andrea Naft*

In Hebrew the word for pure is *bar*, from *barar*. It can mean beloved, empty, choice, clean, clear, or innocent. "Heart" is from the word *lebab*. Its many meanings include inner man, mind, will, and heart. These words remind us that purity dwells within us. Our mind, will, and heart reflect that in our actions and our lives. The pure of heart show us God in the miracles in our daily lives. The pure of heart remind us of God's blessings and the daily miracles that occur around us.

I witnessed these miracles when I started working with Esperanza Center as a volunteer interpreter, and these blessed experiences helped me to connect more deeply with my own ancestry and myself.

The immigrant story is close to my heart. My great uncle Nathan was only a child when he voyaged, unaccompanied, to the United States. His parents feared for him due to the ethnic violence against the Jewish population in Telz, Lithuania, and throughout the area.

Nathan, age fourteen, endured the terrible boat trip. On his last night on the ship, he was robbed of his only two dollars and the address of an aunt with whom he was to live. When he arrived in Manhattan, no one met him because the letter announcing Nathan's travel plans had never arrived. Bewildered and hungry, but with a pure and trusting heart, Nathan climbed out of the roped-off area where the officials put him when no one came for him. He walked north identifying Yiddish speakers and followed them to the Lower East Side. There he began to follow a woman with a basket of fresh rolls draped over her arm who walked like his mother. A miracle unfolded, as it turned out. That woman was his mother's sister.

Much like Great Uncle Nathan and today's children who ride the tops of trains to escape their own country and enter the United States, I have felt a spiritual force leading me to a new place. That new place was my work with unaccompanied immigrant minors.

After retiring from decades of teaching, I found myself in unexpected territory as a white Jewish woman volunteering as a Spanish translator for Catholic Charities. In this role, I heard the quiet voices of mothers and children describing the struggles of crossing borders, of parents trusting to pay guides to bring their beloved children over the border and into their loving arms to safety from gangs and violence. Many of these parents struggled for years to gather the payments by working hard in a strange but safer land.

The first family I worked with for Catholic Charities not only exemplified to me the meaning of "pure of heart," they helped me link their story with mine and my family's. Months earlier in a restaurant, I had met Scott, a pro bono lawyer and coauthor of this book, for whom I provided translation with clients. Scott introduced me to his young clients, Salvadoran brothers Victor and Jorge. Victor, the oldest brother, in his early twenties, had lived in America for several years and was now sponsoring his newly arrived teenage brother, Jorge.

Both young men had fled abuse in Central America at the hands of their father who suffered PTSD and emotional scarring from being forced to kill fellow citizens as a paramilitary soldier in the Salvadoran civil war. The father drank often and became violent with his family. The brothers' oldest sister was the first family member to escape to the United States, where she worked to pay for Victor's escape when he was in his late teens. Victor in turn worked and brought Jorge. The two older siblings worked diligently so the youngest could attend high school.

Victor's warmth, smile, and enthusiasm contrasted dramatically with what I knew of his history. The siblings hid well from the world the scars of their father's abuse, meeting the future with hard work and joy.

Scott's pro bono services guided the family through the long and successful process of gaining a green card for Jorge. Months later, Scott asked Jorge to testify for a bill before the Maryland State Legislature. Since the 1990s, federal immigration law has allowed a special citizenship path for children under age twenty-one if a state juvenile court determined that they had been abused, abandoned, or neglected by a parent. Most states, however, only give jurisdiction to juvenile courts for children under eighteen. The Maryland bill sought to increase to age twenty-one the juvenile court jurisdiction age in order to match the federal immigration law.

My job in the effort to get this bill passed was to coach Jorge with his testimony and to translate for him. Jorge was especially motivated because he knew his older sister, Veronica, might flee El Salvador soon, and she was over eighteen. Perhaps because of this deep love for her, Jorge did not want me to translate for him in the legislative hearing; he wanted to improve his English and speak for himself. He wished to speak directly to his audience. Long hours of pronunciation practice, writing words out in transliteration, and rehearsal ensued.

In Annapolis, on a crisp January day, the state delegates, tired from long hours of testimony and fact-

finding, chatted, snacked, and checked their com-
puters. When Jorge stood to tell his difficult story in
strongly accented English, the room soon quieted. All
eyes turned to him. Here was "a real person"—not just
a thought, or an image, or a news article, or a movie
of a child passing through Guatemala and Mexico on
the tops of trains, or a murderous trip across a desert
to safety. Delegates listened intently. The bill eventually passed and would become active the following
October 1. It felt miraculous to Jorge's team of sup-
porters.

Seasons later, during the Jewish holidays called "The
Days of Awe," Scott and I sat in Baltimore County Cir-
cuit Court for the first custody case under this new law.
We witnessed a miracle that day, too.

Jorge's sister, Veronica, had successfully fled El Salvador and was twenty years old. She had survived un-
speakable parental abuse and made it to the United
States the previous spring. She would turn twenty-one
in five days, so Scott persuaded the judge to schedule
Veronica's hearing in the two days after the law went
into effect and one day before her birthday. Awful
questions were asked of Veronica: "Did your father
abuse you when he was drunk? Did he beat you with
his fists? With belts? Did he try to kill you with his
machete? Did he attempt to hang himself in front of
you?" Veronica became the first person in the state to

benefit from the new law that her younger brother had helped to pass.

Scott, voice and hands shaking, reported to the judge that in thirty years of working with Social Services, this case was truly the worst case of abuse he had encountered. At the end of the court hearing, Scott's eyes were red and puffed. We all had tears in our eyes that day, in the season of the Jewish calendar called the Days of Awe. We hugged, we cried, we laughed. We felt awe. The judge made the determination needed for Veronica's immigration status, and months later, she received her green card.

While I marvel at the miracles with which I have been blessed by these children, I am, at the same time, conscious of all the pain and work that precede and follow these sacred experiences. Victor labored tirelessly in the United States at several jobs in the shadows of his own undocumented status to support his brother and sister when they each arrived. Jorge and Veronica clung to trains, trudged through deserts, and survived personal assault during the dangerous trips here alone. Esperanza staff often work long hours at less-than-private-sector pay to help meet overwhelming needs. The oftentimes bitter fruits of these labors of love are born of sweat and tears, not of magic.

There is a connection between the purity of these children's hearts and the miracles of love that evolve.

Children's purity touches our lives and spurs us to be better people. When we open our hearts in similar vulnerable ways, we will recognize, like young Nathan seeing his mother in his aunt's gait, the connection that we have with others and within ourselves.

Because these miracles are so hard-won, they have helped me to experience compassion that is raw and deep and even divine. It is through the purity of these children's hearts that I have seen God.

## The Depth from Which All Else Springs

*Lord Jesus, what could it mean really to "see God"?*
*Are you suggesting that we might see your Loving Parent*
*as we see our own loving parents (if we are so blessed)?*
*Or do you mean that we will see a Loving Parent*
*in all the life around us,*
*if only we are pure in heart?*
*Or perhaps you mean that those who are pure in heart*
*will begin to see now*
*what one day they will see in the transformed time of eternity*
*the blazing glory of God's own love in the Holy Spirit?*

*Help us, then, Lord, to purity of heart.*
*We know that you do not mean in the first place*
*the ritual purity that was important to your people.*
*And you are not speaking of our sexuality,*
*deeply though it does define us.*
*You mean something at the very center of our lives,*
*the depth from which all else springs,*
*our desires and images and most personal actions.*
*The place without place that is blessedly whole,*
*single in its purpose,*
*longing to be obedient to your covenant love,*
*selfless because we sense that our true selves are only found in you.*
*Like a mother caring for her child,*

*a judge seeking justice,*
*an artist conceiving music to enthrall, console, or transport,*
*the pure of heart are perhaps innocent*
*but they are still more involved,*
*less concerned with what today is called multitasking*
*than with the one task necessary,*
*which you teach us is God's very reign.*
*Are they not what today are called people of integrity?*

*We have seen them, Lord,*
*and can imitate them.*
*As we have first encountered and imitate you.*

—Leo J. O'Donovan, S.J.

# Blessed Are the Refugees

Blessed Are the Peacemakers

# Blessed Are the Peacemakers for They Shall Be Called Children of God

*Andrea Naft*

Who is a peacemaker? Where does making of peace begin? Some go out and make war to bring peace. Others search for reconciliation between people at odds. Inwardly we must make peace with our own actions, with the actions of others, and with forces beyond ourselves. Sometimes the forces outside, or within, seem so insurmountably dark and hopeless that we give way to despair.

The teachings of the Beatitudes tell us that the peacemakers are the children of God. My experience at Esperanza has led me to encounters with young mothers who make great sacrifices and flee the dark and narrow place that promises poverty, death, or sin. They come to the United States so that their own future, and the future of their children, will be filled with good works and a spiritual life full of possibilities. They are both Madonnas and children of God wishing to bring peace to the world of strife into which they have been born.

These mothers radiate beauty. But not the kind Michelangelo evoked in the white marble statue of Mary in the Pieta. These women have dark, straight hair that frames their round young faces. Although often short of stature, these women, aglow with their smiles and intelligent voices, radiate responsibility, strength, and devotion. Some are very young women with sons who are just entering their teenage years. Others are grandmothers with missing teeth, unable to read in Spanish or English, pursuing their dreams so they can help their families. Their hands are roughened from years of labor in fields or in factories. These women have risked their lives to cross borders and save their loved ones. For years, they have sent home money to support their children until the danger became too great for their children and their families. Finally, the children had to leave their native countries.

I have met many such mothers from Central America in the conference rooms of Catholic Charities where I am a volunteer interpreter. The lawyers there learn the women's stories in order to petition the courts to grant them legal custody of their own children or grandchildren. With joy and pride, they have harvested food, cleaned houses, worked in restaurants, or sewn in factories to support their children because jobs, safety, and opportunities no longer exist in their home country. Fighting tears, the women whisper descriptions of physical abuse and abandonment. They journeyed on buses and trains, across several countries, and suffered cold, hungry, sleepless, and dangerous thirty-six-hour desert hikes. They feared the immigration agent who might arrest them. Some guides were trustworthy, others not.

These mothers work long hours at difficult jobs to make money in the United States and send it home to relatives who care for their children. The women hurt from their separation from close-knit Latino families, yet feel blessed with the opportunity to support their loved ones. Once their children turn eleven or twelve, however, the gangs attempt to recruit them. If the children refuse, they and their families are threatened. For some children, this means extortion of money they do not have. For others, beatings or witnessing the killing of uncles, aunts, siblings, and parents. Children move from relative to relative, town to town, seeking safety.

I recall meeting a fourth-grade child who was no longer safe at home with relatives. He had to leave the town to escape violence. He went to work in the coffee fields, suffering cuts from machetes he had to use, enduring twelve-hour days with only one break for food and drink. When the crops were sprayed with pesticides, he was too. When the gangs tried to recruit him, life became so dangerous that the family sent him to his undocumented grandmother in the United States. In school, he became despondent and depressed and then school-phobic. The grandmother despaired and sought help from Catholic Charities, hoping to get him documented and over his fears.

When the choices become too limited or extended family can no longer help, there is no safe place for the children in their home country. They can join a gang, or they can repeat their mother's dangerous trek across borders, searching for safety and reunification. Here in the United States, they hope for blessings. They hope for safety and a return to school. They hope to escape the dangerous life as a gang member. If they are forced to return to their homeland, they will face violence or death—whether they join the gang or not.

Another day, I sat in the conference room with a young woman and her nine-year-old son. They were newly reunited. He hardly knew her. He motionlessly listened to his mother retell her story of abandonment by her partner, lack of money and work, and her journey to the United States to provide for her child. Once here, she sent money home for his support every two weeks. When her parents became too ill to care for her son, she worked even harder to pay the thousands of dollars to hire a "guide" to take him north. She felt great anxiety about his safety, but she felt some comfort when he called each night by cell phone. After reaching the border successfully, he was apprehended, put in a holding cell, transferred to a safe home, and finally, with the help of Catholic Charities, he was reunited with the mother he barely knew.

She hoped to gain full custody of her son and a citizenship path for him. Her porcelain gold-rimmed teeth shone in her warm smile. With a modest income from working in a mushroom factory, she planned to work more hours or jobs to pay court fees for her custody plea and her child's green card fees. So much money, but she will earn it.

She was twenty-eight, the age of my son. His generation went to college; her generation left grade school to work. There was no other option. The fathers suffered from PTSD and turned to alcohol after surviving civil war injustices, family members disappearing, violence, death, and poverty.

The lawyer left the room to copy the many documents of birth and life that the courts demand. We chatted.

"You must be so happy to have your son here."

"Yes. I am so fortunate. Yet I am so scared for all the mothers here, separated from their children. Border enforcement has changed. If they go to see their children, they will not be able to return here to work. Their families will not survive. It breaks my heart."

She playfully whispered something to her son. She was the Madonna with her child.

Blessed indeed are these women. Their generous hearts heal fear and divisiveness. May we be so blessed to witness and learn from the peacemakers among us who daily sacrifice. These Madonnas are both the mothers of humanity and the children of God.

## The True Daughters and Sons of God

*Since the end of World War II, Lord,*
*we human beings have all stood under the threat*
*of the nuclear power*
*that we ourselves have created.*
*It is now in the hands of not just a few but in fact many nations.*
*Our world is truly threatened by satanic suicide.*
*An equally satanic struggle to have as much*
 *of this power as possible*
*wreaks economic havoc above all on the poor of the world,*
*who are deprived of resources that could support them*
*but that go instead to producing more weapons.*

*Where are the peacemakers, Lord, where?*
*Look around, you tell us.*
*In fact, there are many peacemakers—*
*men and women throughout the world*
*who have heeded your call to make peace:*
*Dorothy Day in America, Simone Weil in France,*
*all the conscientious objectors like Franz Jägerstätter in Austria*
*who have refused to serve in wars they considered unjust.*
*Whole movements such as Pax Christi have pledged*
*to end all war and "make peace."*

*Among the voices who are not pacifist in the full sense of the term,*

## BLESSED ARE THE REFUGEES

*Pope John XXIII and his encyclical "Pacem in Terris"*
*have a certain pride of place.*
*Pope Paul VI surely ranks high with his teaching*
*that "development is the new name for peace,"*
*and our current Pope Francis has urged a radical reconsideration*
*of whether traditional just-war thinking is applicable*
*in the contemporary world of devastating weaponry.*

*You told us long ago that it is the peacemakers*
*who will be called the true daughters and sons of God.*
*And you meant "peace" in the full sense your people gave it,*
*shalom, the full wellbeing of all.*
*Does this mean that we will not be blessed or happy*
*or be your brothers and sisters*
*unless our lives are dedicated not just to avoiding war*
*but indeed to making peace?*
*I shudder, Lord, at how clear the answer is*

—Leo J. O'Donovan, S.J.

# Blessed Are They Who Are Persecuted for the Sake of Righteousness, for Theirs Is the Kingdom of Heaven

*Scott Rose*

His feet were bound, his head bowed, surrendered to the pain and power of persecution.

I was as shaken as he was. It was Juan's first day of what, to our shock and dismay later, would turn out to be a two-year incarceration for pushing a classmate in Maryland's Prince George's County. Neither of us could speak the other's language. He just kept motioning to me, tearfully, that he wanted a hug. I gave him a quick embrace. His leg irons clanked in the emptiness.

From the beginning, I knew this boy was not an oppressor. But it took me several years to realize that neither was the legal system that overly prosecuted him. His persecutors were the drug cartel and gangs in El Salvador that hunted him and a vicious rape when he

# Blessed Are the Refugees

Blessed Are They Who Are Persecuted

was eight years old that haunted him. This persecution drove him from El Salvador into a U.S. jail—nowhere near the kingdom of heaven that Jesus promised in his Sermon on the Mount.

I first met Juan several years before, representing him in a Prince George's County court. He was emotionless, due to what I then thought was shyness but later realized was depression. Juan's father had abandoned the boy when he was one year old and died soon after. Juan's mother had used excessive discipline. Fearing for his life, the boy had fled El Salvador because the drug cartel was killing Salvadoran boys to keep them from joining gangs that had become barriers to the cartel's business. Juan had successfully avoided recruitment by the gangs but became hunted by the cartel. Emblematic of the chaos in El Salvador, Juan was threatened simultaneously by bad guys on both sides. So he fled, alone, to the United States, was detained at the border, and placed with his aunt in Prince George's County, pending deportation proceedings.

After a successful first step in a Prince George's County Circuit Court, we applied for his green card. Several months from receiving it, Juan made a mistake that jeopardized his entire future. Depressed and lonely, he hung out with a classmate who had a connection to a Prince George's County gang. While not a member of the gang, the friend was being recruited to join, and he kept trying to persuade Juan to join with him. Juan kept declining. (Two years later, the prosecutor would write a letter to the immigration judge acknowledging that Juan had been telling the truth that he was not a gang member.)

One day, in one event, the friend started fighting with a classmate and drew Juan into participating. Juan assisted by pushing the boy several times. But Juan was surprised and scared when his friend pulled out a knife and stole the classmate's cell phone. Juan, who had just turned eighteen, was charged as an adult accomplice to armed robbery, even though police acknowledged that he had never touched the knife or the cell phone and the victim had not been hurt. In Juan's mind and heart, the incident was a schoolyard fight, not a crime.

It wasn't until several years later—when I learned of his childhood rape and the resulting PTSD—that I realized why Juan had been unable to say no to his friend initially or to walk away when things escalated. Like many trauma survivors, Juan froze emotionally and physically in stressful situations, and he was especially triggered by people who resembled his perpetrator. Juan was manipulated and intimidated by his friend, who was of similar size and age to the male cousin who had raped him.

Because Juan had associated with a person who had associated with a gang, the prosecutor wouldn't talk about a reasonable plea bargain, and the federal immigration agency reinitiated deportation proceedings. The jail bond was set so high that Juan's family couldn't afford it.

Matters became more complex when the system started to use the criminal charges as leverage to persuade Juan to provide information for a gang investigation in Prince George's County. Juan tried to help, but he had no significant information because he wasn't a gang member, as was later confirmed. Regardless, the prosecutors kept delaying plea discussions and asking for trial continuances to give more time for the gang investigation to proceed. Days in jail turned into weeks, and then months. All because Juan pushed a classmate.

Meanwhile, Juan's mental health deteriorated. With assistance from volunteer interpreters, I discovered that Juan was having intense nightmares and was receiving death threats from inmates who found out he was cooperating with law enforcement, even though he didn't have any significant information. Juan was being persecuted for doing the right thing.

At one point, Juan admitted to me that he had suicidal thoughts, so I requested his transfer to the medical unit for suicide watch. (I was even more worried about his being hurt by others.) After a week, the jail planned to return him to the same cell block, so I intervened again to get him transferred to a protective custody area.

During Juan's long incarceration, I prayed a lot about justice. When I first learned of the fight that jeopardized all the work I had done for Juan, I was so frustrated with him that I considered not helping him anymore. I changed my mind, however, when I reflected on Jesus' command to us to visit the prisoner and welcome the immigrant (the more descriptive meaning of the Greek word for "stranger"):

> "[f]or I was hungry and you gave me food, I was thirsty and you gave me something to drink, I was a stranger and you welcomed me, I was naked and you gave me clothing, I was sick and you took care of me, I was in prison and you visited me." Then the righteous will answer him, "Lord, when was it that we saw you hungry and gave you food, or thirsty and gave you something to drink? And when was it that we saw you a stranger and welcomed you, or naked and gave you clothing? And when was it that we saw you sick or in prison and visited you?" And the king shall answer them, "Truly I tell you, just as you did it to one of the least of these who are members of my family, you did it to me." (Matt 25:35-41)

I realized that the refugee children whom Esperanza serves, like Juan, meet most of the categories of suffering people Jesus calls us to help—they are strangers, they are thirsty and hungry when they cross the border, they experience imprisonment in border detention facilities, and while they may not be ill, many, like Juan, suffer from trauma-related mental health issues. Indeed, Jesus was a refugee child, his parents fleeing with him from Bethlehem to Egypt to escape violence from Herod (Matt 2:13-14).

I knew that abandoning Juan because he had gotten harder to love would have been as unrighteous as the trauma that haunted him.

We all know that few people are at their best when they are in pain. Yet, often when we consider helping others, we want to skip over those who act out in their suffering because they are difficult to love and we don't like the discomfort of being around their pain. Or we blame them because it is easier to feel anger than sadness. Instead of grieving about the poverty and violence that have driven immigrants to our border, we condemn them for our unemployment rate or our crime statistics. We hold immigrant children responsible by blaming their parents or their countries that neglected them.

After I moved beyond faulting Juan, I blamed the legal system that overly prosecuted him. As I had more contact with the detective and the prosecutors, however, I grew to respect them. I realized that they were trying to do the right thing and that they shared a common goal with Juan and me in preventing gangs from coercing vulnerable boys. I was impressed that one of the prosecutors followed through on his promise to provide assistance to Juan in his immigration case a year later.

Then I refocused my anger onto the gangs, but that didn't make me feel less sad for Juan. It also didn't help me to blame the older male cousin who had raped Juan. Most likely, the cousin was acting out in response to his own past sexual trauma.

I even considered not including Juan's story in this book for fear that his one mistake might perpetuate inaccurate misperceptions and fears despite the fact that the overwhelming majority of Esperanza's children lead exemplary lives. Not sharing the more complex pain of refugee children, however, would rob readers of the graced opportunity to experience love more profoundly.

Juan spent a year in a Prince George's County jail for the state criminal charges, finally getting a conviction of a low-level misdemeaner for pushing. He was immediately transferred to another detention center for the immigration case and spent another year there. Heather, a brilliant and persistent managing attorney at Esperanza, worked tirelessly to represent Juan, and it was in that long trial preparation process that Juan disclosed to me that he had been raped as a child..

In Juan's case, the righteous outcome would have been for the federal government to dismiss the deportation proceedings and, instead, approve his original application for a green card, given the minor nature of his offense, the excessive period he spent in jail, his repeated refusal to succumb to coercion by gangs, his life-endangering cooperation with the gang investigation, and his tragic background. But that did not happen.

Due to a combination of Heather's skilled dedication, the immigration judge's compassion, and many prayers from the Esperanza community, the court did permit a compromise, granting Juan an order withholding deportation. This meant that Juan would not be deported to sure danger in El Salvador as long as he maintained a responsible life, but it also prevented Juan from becoming a U.S. citizen and receiving government assistance should he need it. Despite the bittersweet outcome, we were thrilled that Juan would finally be released and that he would be safe. The conclusion wasn't righteous, but Juan would be free. It was clear to everyone who had contact with him, including the detention staff, that Juan had become a model for others—deeply religious and prayerful, truly remorseful for his past mistakes, and sincerely committed to a positive future of caring and contribution.

Several months after Juan was released, I took him to a Spanish-language Mass near his aunt's house where he lived. I was thrilled to be with Juan outside of a jail and to celebrate with him sacramentally the joy of his release and new life. I felt in awe of his strength and resilience that had enabled him to overcome so many challenges, but I could also see in his tired eyes that the past two years had wounded him deeply. I began to feel overwhelmed with the pervasiveness of trauma in this young man's life and my inability to protect him.

Minutes later, though, I was moved and inspired to hear the day's Gospel, Matthew 25:35-40, the same passage that had prevented me from abandoning Juan after the fight, where Jesus calls us to welcome the immigrant and visit the prisoner. I realized that in the Scripture Jesus focuses solely on helping suffering people; he doesn't spend any time attributing blame. Certainly not on the individuals themselves—including even prisoners. Neither does he condemn the people or systems that cause the suffering. And he doesn't tell us we have to be skilled enough to fix any of it. We don't have to cure those who are ill, just comfort them. We aren't supposed to judge the imprisoned, just visit them. We don't need to determine U.S. immigration policy, just be kind to immigrants. Similarly, with this Beatitude, we shouldn't focus on identifying persecutors, just love and learn from the persecuted.

During the exchange of peace, I hugged Juan and whispered clumsily in his ear, "*Paz, mi hijo*" ("Peace, my son"). I hoped that our embrace of peace and the Body of Christ he received were small signs of the kingdom of heaven that Jesus had promised him in the Beatitudes.

## Witnesses Worthy of the Kingdom

*Lord, how strange a thing is your praise of persecution!*
*How much more readily we think of the many women and men,*
*canonized or not,*
*whom we call saints and think of as models for our lives,*
*witnesses worthy of the kingdom—*
*the coming full reign and glory of your God, the Holy One.*

*And yet from the earliest centuries,*
*we know that the martyrs of the church,*
*those who under persecution gave their very lives*
*in faithfulness to the gospel,*
*were considered the greatest of saints—*
*often venerated in a category almost beyond sainthood itself.*
*We recall them in our longest Eucharistic prayer.*
*Many of us are named after them:*
*Stephen and Damian, Catherine and Agnes, Lawrence and Lucy.*
*They are our noblest witnesses from the earliest days of the church.*

*And somehow, Lord, we overlook the fact*
*that many men and women of our own time have been persecuted,*
*and indeed martyred, for their faith.*
*Under the Nazis in Germany, martyrs of faith*
*such as Maximilian Kolbe, Aloys Andritzki,*
*and Jesuit Alfred Delp.*

## Blessed Are the Refugees

*In the bloody 1980s in El Salvador alone,*
*martyrs included the six Jesuits*
*of the University of Central America,*
*their housekeeper and her daughter;*
*Archbishop Oscar Romero;*
*four American women greatly influenced by him—*
*Maura Clarke, Ita Ford, Dorothy Kazel, and Jean Donovan;*
*and the young Jesuit Rutilio Grande,*
*the first to be assassinated in that country.*

*The catalogue of martyrs continued woefully*
*in the last years of the twentieth century and into our own.*
*The Trappist monks of Tibhirine in Algeria;*
*Ritchie Fernandez, S.J., in Cambodia;*
*the community of the Adorers of the Precious Blood in Liberia;*
*the beloved Sr. Leonella Sgorbati in Somalia.*
*Indeed, Lord, as Fr. Grande said,*
*"It is a dangerous thing to be a Christian in our world."*

*What precious names these are!*
*And what blessing it bears to recall them,*
*to learn their story,*
*to appreciate their sacrifice.*
*Help us to share such faith, Lord Jesus.*
*Help us to realize that it may differ certainly in intensity*
*but is the same in kind,*
*a trust in you and your Father in the Holy Spirit*

*Blessed Are They Who Are Persecuted*

*whom we are called to cooperate with and surrender to
if the kingdom of heaven is to be ours too.*

—Leo J. O'Donovan, S.J.

75

BLESSED ARE THE REFUGEES

REJOICE AND BE GLAD

# Rejoice and Be Glad

*Scott Rose*

In the conclusion to his teaching on the Beatitudes, Jesus addresses his disciples in a direct and startling way: "Blessed are you when people revile you and persecute you and utter all kinds of evil against you falsely on my account. Rejoice and be glad, for your reward is great in heaven" (Matt 5:11-12). Here the Lord is warning but also encouraging the disciples—and us as well—that their witness to him will entail the same kind of sacrifice and suffering that was the lot of the prophets. And yet the disciples should "rejoice and be glad"—for their "reward will be great in heaven."

How can these words of the prophet who fulfills all prophecy guide us in our response to refugee youth?

We will be blessed when we choose to comfort and heal these children, especially when this love requires sacrifice. In the context of the Beatitudes, such response will be because of Jesus as he called us to honor the marginalized. In the context of Jesus's parable of the Great Judgment (Matt 25:31-46), helping refugee children will be *for* Jesus as he is present in the marginalized, including the immigrant.

This concept of multiple motivations for caring for young immigrants commends itself all the more at the end of a book filled with stories of children facing great challenges. What is more difficult to grasp is how to rejoice and feel glad. The tragedies that drove these children to flee from their countries continue to haunt them despite life-saving refuge in the United States. The fact that in eternity they will see God, inherit the earth, or experience the kingdom of heaven is not sufficient consolation to many of us, nor is the possibility that we, their comforters, might find some reward there as well. From time to time, though, we do find joy when we see that their burden is less and that they feel hope.

For Maria, who was poor in spirit, her past sexual trauma led to her being exploited by an older man in the United States. But she found the strength to end the relationship, she is close to receiving her green card, she found a job cleaning houses, and her father, who had abandoned her, has continued to seek reconciliation with her. For this, we are glad.

Williams continues to mourn for Adan, and now for his aging mother in El Salvador who is being abused by his father. Williams is a permanent legal citizen of the United States, he recently got a raise at his restaurant job, he is making plans to attend community college next year, and he appeared on national television to share his story and advocate for immigration reform. For this, we rejoice.

Juan, who was persecuted, recently aged out of a special Medicaid program. As a result, he lost coverage to pay for the psychotropic medication he so desperately needs. But he recently got a job painting houses, and a local clinic found a special fund to purchase medicine for him. For this, we are glad.

After the presentation of the Beatitudes in Matthew's Gospel, Jesus speaks of the witness of his disciples: "You are the salt of the earth" (Matt 5:13), charging them with the awesome responsibility *to be* the salt of the earth. We also rejoice when we witness ordinary people being the salt of the earth, extending extraordinary kindness to the children we met in this book.

One Sunday, after preaching a sermon about refugee children, I was deluged with offers of volunteer help. I appreciated it greatly and I believed people's earnestness, but I assumed that their enthusiasm would fade, especially since I didn't have the time or energy to organize and support them. To my surprise, they persisted with their offers to help.

One older couple emailed me several times, proposing to buy Christmas gifts for some of the children. When the woman matter-of-factly stated that she wanted to take care of youth *in her community,* I was so moved. To her, these strangers were her neighbors. For two Advent seasons, the couple has spent time and money buying and delivering gifts.

A younger woman caught me at Mass several times to remind me that she wanted to help as an interpreter. For weeks, she drove a long distance to transport a boy to the studio of a local artist, another volunteer, who was helping the hulking teenager pursue his passion. I was touched one day when she bought the boy a drawing kit. I was overjoyed with one sacred moment when the interpreter and the artist modeled praying hands for the religious drawing the boy wanted to create. The interpreter, a Catholic, and the artist, an atheist, helped this boy, so pure of heart, to see God.

Two older women contacted me repeatedly with their plan to organize access to English classes for youth over eighteen. Even more impressive, using interpreters over the phone, they creatively persisted in engaging and persuading the insecure teenagers to join the classes. They even provided transportation. I tear up when I imagine one of those Miss Daisy-like ladies in the front seat of her car, chauffeuring a nineteen-year-old Latino boy in the back—in utter silence because she couldn't speak a word of Spanish. This pure love, for a moment, turned the world upside down.

All of these ordinary people who offer extraordinary tenderness are truly the salt of the earth. Perhaps the same earth that Jesus promises the meek will inherit someday.

Jesus goes on to tell his disciples that they are the light of the world and a city on a mountain that cannot be hidden (Matt 5:14). Catholic social teaching emphasizes that countries with more resources have a greater responsibility to welcome and care for immigrants. Individually we can be the salt of the earth. As a nation, the United States is called to be a light of the world. These children flee to us for the refuge we can provide, and we should embrace that honor and responsibility with grace.

As with most refugee children from Central America, Maria crossed the border at night, guided toward lights in the United States. And our light has continued to be a source of comfort. As a child who was raped repeatedly, she endured terrifying dreams every night. She couldn't turn on a light because she shared a bedroom with others, so she would just sit at the edge of her bed and cry. Her nightmares have continued in the United States but with much less frequency. And, because of our country's resources, she now has a bedroom of her own, and she dispels the nightmares when they come by turning on a light and reading her Bible.

Juan's nightmares from his past trauma have also become less frequent. For the two years in jail, he tried to stay awake at night and sleep during the day so that when he had nightmares, he could wake to light. Now, he is able to sleep in the dark—with the help of a night-light in his aunt's downstairs den where he lives.

When Williams journeyed to the United States several years ago, he crossed the border in early dawn. He describes walking toward the United States with light from the dim sunrise showing him a goal to strive toward as well as guiding each step in his path. One simple joy in his life now is playing soccer video games with his nephew, the boy who Williams's brother, Adan, lost his life rescuing in the ocean. I delight in the image of those two Salvadoran refugee boys, alone but safe at night in the basement of a cramped Baltimore townhouse, bonding and healing by the light of a television.

The Sermon on the Mount comes from the great central section of Matthew's Gospel on Jesus's preaching and teaching in Galilee. As the evangelist later begins in chapter 19 to narrate the journey to Jerusalem, he includes the lovely story, common to Mark and Luke as well, of Jesus commanding his disciples to let children come to him, and not to hinder them. The staff of Esperanza Center and Jesuit Refugee Service believe Jesus is making the same demand today of all of us in the United States: let the children come.

We are honored and glad for the opportunity to respond to Jesus's call, and we rejoice with the thousands of refugee children who have made a home in the United States and contributed to their communities— and the millions of other Americans who find their own ways to support these children and learn from them.

**Blessed Are the Refugees, for They Are the Presence of God**

*O dear God, are you holding your head in your hands,*
*helpless before the horror of all the refugees and displaced people*
*in your world today?*
*The long line of refugees crossing hillcrest after hillcrest,*
*hoping for a home.*
*The overcrowded and often foundering boats of families fleeing*
*across the seas.*
*The children running through the night to escape the brutalities*
*of Central America's Northern Triangle, all the while prey*
*to coyotes and cartels.*

*Good God, it is the equivalent of the whole population*
*of Great Britain.*
*We have seen nothing like it since World War II.*
*Have you?*
*What is your answer?*

*Good God, give us an answer.*
*Forgive the anger in our voices.*
*Yes, forgive us.*
*But it is there.*
*Still more, though: our plea for help for these millions and millions*
*of your own children, the brothers and sisters of your Word to us,*
*our own, "our own refugees,"*

*surely as dear to you as any of us in the comfort of the north.*

*But you are silent.*
*So perhaps we are the ones not truly paying attention.*
*Might that be?*
*Perhaps you do not have an answer but a presence nevertheless.*
*Perhaps Pope Francis has given us the clue*
*when he said in Bangladesh,*
*"The presence of God today is also called Rohingya."*
*Perhaps your presence is also called Maria, and Adan and*
*Williams, Sofia and Gabriela, Camila and Elena, Nathan,*
*Victor and Jorge, Juan.*

*Show us where you are among us, O merciful God.*
*Let us see truly the homeless who hope in you*
*and in your Word to us.*
*Let us see the Lord you have given us to bring us together,*
*to help us be one, a human family, the community of Christ*
*in the Spirit.*
*Forgive us if we are angry now at ourselves.*
*Ease our hearts as you open our eyes to see you in our refugees.*
*Surely then we will know what to do.*

—Leo J. O'Donovan, S.J.

# About the Organizations

**Esperanza Center,** a program of Catholic Charities of Baltimore, is a comprehensive nonprofit immigrant resource center that offers hope and essential services to thousands of immigrants each year from 150 different countries. Services include immigration legal services, medical and dental care, and English as a Second Language education.

To learn more, to volunteer, or to donate, contact esperanzainfo@cc-md.org or visit www.catholiccharities-md.org/services/esperanza-center/.

**Jesuit Refugee Service** is an international Catholic organization serving refugees and other forcibly displaced people. Founded as a work of the Society of Jesus (Jesuits) in 1980, in direct response to the humanitarian crisis of the Vietnamese boat people, JRS today works in fifty-one countries worldwide to meet the educational, health, and social needs of more than 750,000 refugees.

To learn more, to volunteer, or to donate, visit www.jrsusa.org.

# About the Artists

**Ana Silvia Herrera Delgado**, who goes by Silvia, is a twenty-two-year-old refugee who fled from El Salvador when she was nineteen to escape gang violence. Abandoned by both of her parents when she was three months old, Silvia was raised by her grandmother in poverty, frequently hungry. Assisted by Esperanza Center, she is now a permanent legal resident of the United States, has a job, and sings in the choir of her Catholic parish in Maryland.

**Jose Enrique Portillo Delgado** is Silvia's nineteen-year-old brother who lives in El Salvador. Raised in poverty, Enrique was forced to quit school after the ninth grade so that he could help support his family who lives each day in fear of gangs that constantly roam the streets. To minimize his exposure, Enrique ventures from his house only to his work during the week and to Sunday Mass. He earns ten dollars per day as an auto mechanic, working ten-hour days, six days per week. His life in El Salvador is so difficult that he wants to migrate to the United States but can't because his family needs him.

# About the Authors

**Mikhael H. Borgonos** is a managing attorney at the Esperanza Center's Immigration Legal Services. His experience includes serving at the Civil Division, Office of Immigration Litigation, and the Antitrust Division, National Criminal Enforcement Section, of the U.S. Department of Justice in Washington, D.C. An immigrant himself, Mikhael is a native of the Philippines and now a naturalized U.S. citizen.

**Andrea Naft** is a volunteer Spanish interpreter for Esperanza Center. She was a public school teacher and private school administrator and is a volunteer tutor at Cuernavaca Kids in Mexico. As a recipient of a Fulbright-Hayes Scholarship to do research in Mexico, she developed curriculum on Mexican culture and history. The grandchild of Russian immigrants who fled persecution, Andrea writes from the perspectives of being Jewish and having family who were refugees.

**Leo J. O'Donovan, S.J.,** is president emeritus of Georgetown University and a past president of the Catholic Theological Society of America. Before serving at Georgetown, he was professor of systematic theology at Weston School of Theology in Cambridge, Massachusetts. Serving now as director of mission for Jesuit Refugee Service/USA, he resides in New York City and publishes in both theology and art criticism.

**Cary Plamondon** is a pro bono attorney with Esperanza Center. She worked for a large Washington, D.C., legal firm for ten years, practicing white-collar defense and health care law. She is a member of several nonprofit boards and serves as a volunteer for the Court Appointed Special Advocate Program. She has a special interest in supporting foster care youth who are transitioning to independent living, and is helping establish a new nonprofit organization to help bridge this gap.

**Scott Rose** is a permanent deacon in the Archdiocese of Baltimore, assigned to Esperanza as a pro bono attorney. He has a special interest in serving immigrant children with trauma histories, inspired by his work in the mental health field, his first job as a child abuse investigator, and his current employment as CEO of a multicounty nonprofit mental health organization.

**Valerie Twanmoh** has been the director of Catholic Charities Esperanza Center since 2011. She came to the center after a twenty-five-year career as a trial attorney and four years serving as deputy state director for a U.S. senator. She serves as a member of various nonprofit and school advisory boards in the Baltimore area. In addition to her role as the center's director, she individually represents immigrant children served by Esperanza.